DEDICATION

This is a story of a horse named Jackson Day, and his ability to overcome many medical challenges. Our book is dedicated to children with health or other life difficulties.

Jackson wants these children to know what you can't do can be overcome by what you can do. This book shows how we can all find fun and new adventures even when life's hardships get in the way.

"Life's limitations can lead to new achievements."

I'm Jackson Day

and I'm Here to Stay

The True Story of a Medically Challenged Horse Who Found Fun, Friends and Fame

by Jacki Day and Jan Janette

Welcome To Your New World, Jackson

Jackson opened his eyes for the first time in the ranch pasture. He was welcomed by his horse and human Mothers as well as his animal friends. These friends and many more would become part of his life forever.

It's OK To Be Different But Sometimes It's Hard

It was obvious from birth that Jackson was not a "pretty" horse. His ears were too big, his head too large, his back and neck were too long, he had buck teeth, his legs were crooked and his feet would always need special shoes.

His First Year Was Filled With Serious Medical Problems

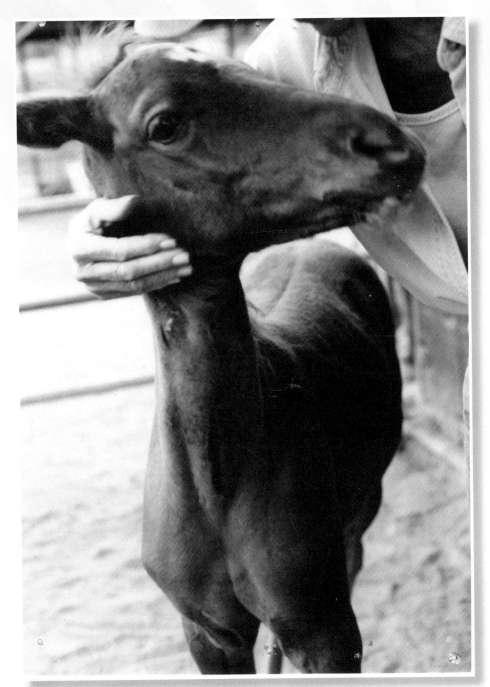

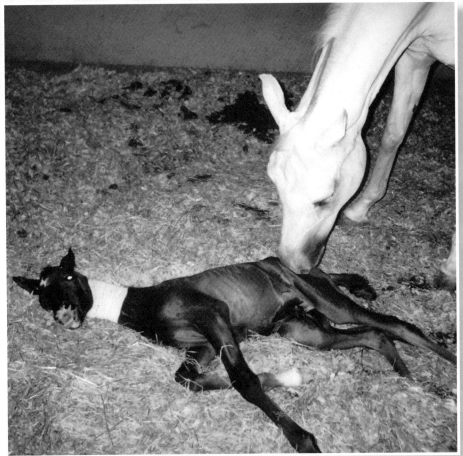

Jackson spent his first weeks in the horse hospital and both Moms stayed with him. He needed blood transfusions within hours of his birth and 2 days later got pneumonia.

Finally Home From The Hospital

Giving Mom A Big Kiss

No More Dirt For Me

As soon as he came home to the ranch he was ready to explore his surroundings and decided that dirt was delicious. Little did he know that eating dirt caused him to have bad poops. Jackson had to wear a special basket on his face to stop that bad habit. In a few weeks he had good poops again and felt much better.

To know Jackson is to love him. It was hard to notice when he wasn't feeling well because he always seemed to be happy. Even when he was alone he entertained himself by using whatever was handy for a toy.

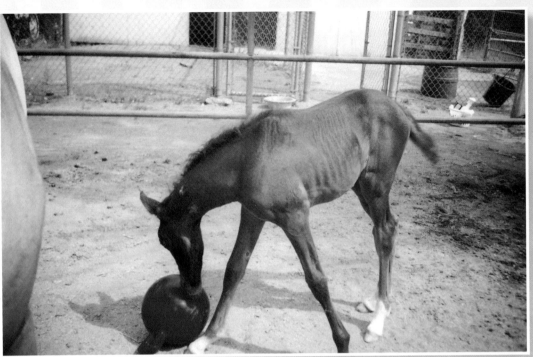

Am I Supposed To Kick The Ball?

Mom, You Missed With The Fly Mask

I Thought I Could Jump Over It

Jackson Is Always Fun To Be With

What Jackson liked most was playing with his many friends, both animal and human. It's very true that no one likes to be around a grump. Although Jackson was in constant discomfort and nasty-tasting medicines and shots were part of his daily life, he always had a happy whinny, bright eyes, and a playful attitude.

OK Let's Race!!

Oh Yes, Right There, That's The Spot!

A Kiss For My Special Friend

6

The Girls Adore Me

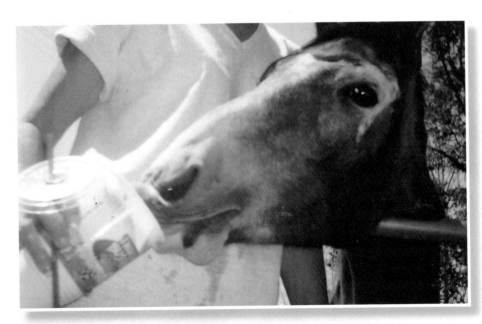

I Want A Drink Too!

Running With Friends: One Of My Favorite Things

Grooming Is Good But Baths: Not One Of My Favorite Things

Friends

Hats Taste Good!

Watch'a Doin'?

I Want To Go In The Car Too!

Mommy(s) and Me

My Glow—In—The—Dark Circle

Even though Jackson was born dark he was going to be a white horse just like his Mom. That change can take up to 10 years. But by the age of 6 months it seemed Jackson's change had already started when a large white circle appeared around his eye. Instead, it was discovered this was a painless skin condition called "Arabian Fading Syndrome." The fun side was that the circle glowed in the dark... sort of like Rudolph's nose.

Jackson's Color Changes

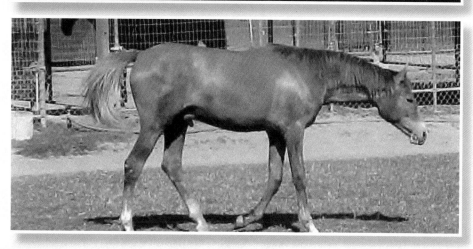

Dressing Up In Costume: Another Of My Favorite Things

Jackson has costumes for many holidays and others just for fun. Some people object to dressing-up animals but he loves attention and is always more than willing to show off for an audience.

Hollywood Will Surely Call

Dress-Up Is Fun!

This Is My "Out Of The Hospital" Dance

Jackson
The
Unicorn

Uncle Sam
Needs Me

15

Jackson Day
For President

I Can Make My
Own Costume

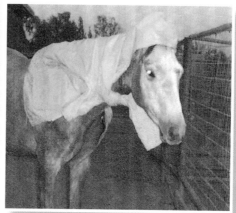

Who Said It Was
Going To Rain?

Is This Bag For Candy Or Carrots?

Sunglasses Make The Outfit

Birthday Parties: Another Of My Favorite Things

Jackson's friends decided to have a party for his first birthday. He and his guests had a fun day, but no one knew what was to come for this brave little horse.

Birthday Carrot Cake

My Birthday Suit

My Fan Club At The Party

Trying To Open My Birthday Presents

"Reading" My Birthday Cards

A few weeks after the birthday party while Jackson was learning to pull a cart, he began to stumble and fall. At first, everyone thought he was just clumsy. Sadly, it continued so off we went to see the doctor. The doctors discovered he had a very serious problem that would require an operation and metal braces in his neck.

Learning To Drive

Back In The Hospital: Visitors Welcome

After Jackson came home, his scheduled recovery time went from 3 to 6 months because he got very sick with an infection and high fevers. This required more medicine and more shots.

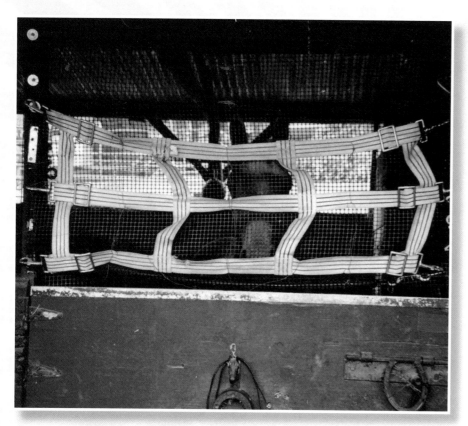

Mom, I Can't Get To My Toys

But leave it to Jackson; he kept his cool and created his own fun. He did not like the screen on his door, but it was necessary because anything within reach became his toy.

This was a bad time for Jackson, but it never kept him from enjoying his friends. Even when he was hurting he always welcomed visitors and remained in high spirits.

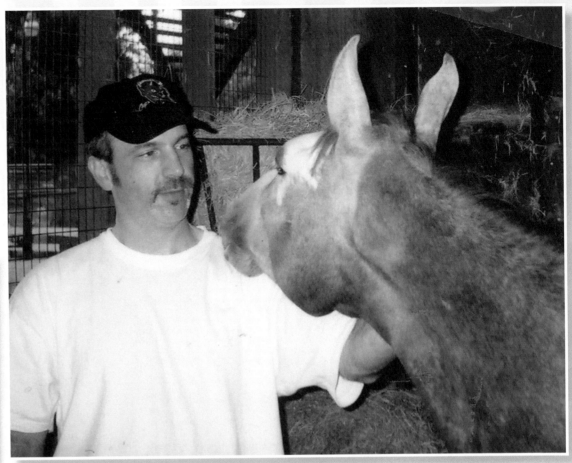

My Best Buddy: Tin Jackson

During his confinement Jackson found a special friend named Tin Jackson. He looked like a real horse, but some thought of him as a toy. The two Jacksons did fun things together like dressing in holiday costumes. They also had secret talks late at night.

Tin Jackson

Happy Valentine's Day

Merry Christmas To You

It's The 4th Of July

Here Comes Peter Cottontail

22

The operation was only a partial success because there was some permanent damage and the doctors said he could never be ridden. This was sad news but a horse like Jackson would find other fun activities that he could do.

There Go My Friends For A Ride

x

With more training, Jackson became very good at pulling a cart. This provided him with mental and physical activity that was exercise and FUN. Since he was one of the only horses at the ranch trained to do this, he gave his human friends rides, was in many parades, and always led the neighborhood Christmas caroling.

Neighborhood Rides

Memorial Day

Ready to Drive

Christmas Parade

Although Jackson was doing well pulling his cart, it soon became obvious that his crooked legs needed attention, so he had to go back to the doctor for another operation. Once again it meant more shots, more medicines and more doctor visits.

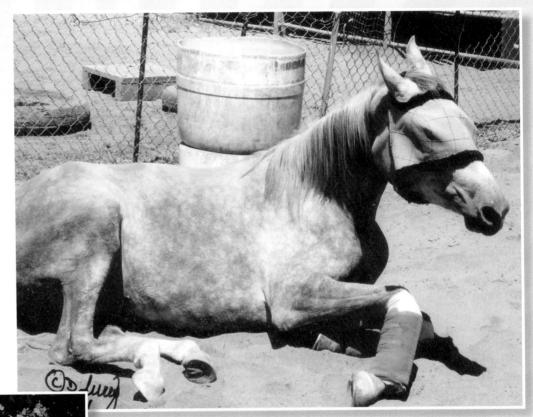

Mom Made Me Rest A Lot

My "Bandages" Made My Friends Want Pink Leggings

Marilyn

Then Jackson met Marilyn, another special friend. He thought Marilyn was really cute! Luckily, she and Tin Jackson also became friends. Marilyn sometimes even dressed up with them.

Happy Halloween

4th of July

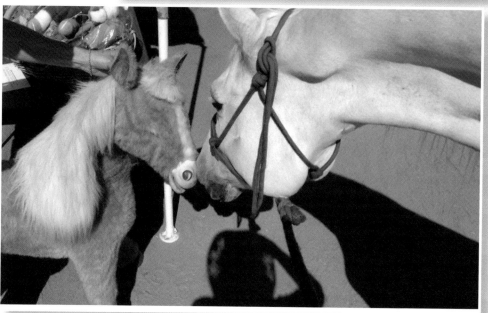

Hi Cutie, I Think You're Special!

Happy Birthday

Because Jackson was able to overcome his disabilities and accomplish so much, his confidence grew. He thought, "I can even compete in shows and do well." AND HE DID

Obstacle Course

Driving Show

This Is Scary But I'm Brave

"These Are A Few Of My Other Talents"

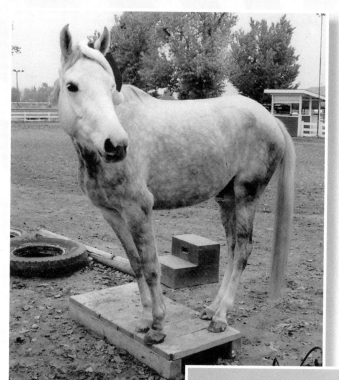

On Board

Smiling

"Once Upon A Time"

Dancing

Singing "E I E I O"

Bowing

Jackson Has Many Jobs At The Ranch

THIS CERTIFICATE ENTITLES

SELAH RANCH
11314 MORENO AVENUE
LAKESIDE CA 92040

TOM SCHAEFER 619.301.3106
LYNDA SCHAEFER 619.701.8154

TO

ONE DRIVING LESSON
WITH THE WORLD
FAMOUS, PATRIOTIC
Jackson Day
PULLING THE CART

AUTHORIZED BY:

Teacher

Greeter

Official Mascot

Helper

Jackson is 17 years old now and will never be considered healthy but with his positive attitude and joy in life, he remains very happy. He is constantly making new friends and discovering new activities.

HIS LIFE IS FULL!

Rolling In The Dirt Is Heaven

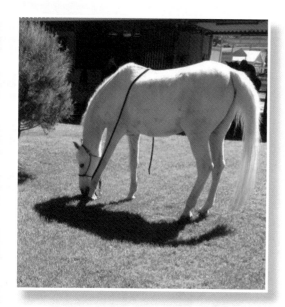

Grass Is My Candy

For Our 9/11 Patriots

Peek-A-Boo

A Smile And A Happy Heart Always Makes Things Better

The End

Acknowledgments

I will attempt to mention most of the special people who have had a positive effect on Jackson's life and provided support each and every day. Not only support for Jackson but for his family as well.

Marjorie Riding, Tom and Lynda Schaefer, Judy Consolin, Kam Wilson, Jennifer Oeland, and all the Riding and Selah Ranch boarders who tolerate his special needs. My personal support team, Jackie Serrano, Jan Janette, Debbie Furry (his special auntie) and my daughter, Lisa Mercer who were always on call. My long-time friends, Patricia Erikson, Cassi Fay and my husband, Tony Day, who provided my emotional support. Also, the ranch crew and boarders who visit him daily.

A special mention to ECLAP veterinarians who have seen him through many health issues and for their patience with an over-protective mom. Also to Jason Harmeson, his farrier who has managed to keep him upright all these years.

Heartfelt appreciation and gratitude to all these people who have given and continue to give to my Jackson Day. With his health issues, six months was all we hoped for but year after year he has beat the odds and is living a happy life.

A very special thank you to Tom Schaefer, the cowboy who calls Jackson "Dude". Tom has always been a major part of his daily life. He is Jackson's friend, his mentor, care-giver and who claims that Jackson has the biggest heart of any horse he's ever known. This from a "cowboy" who prefers western riding but proudly drives a cart with this Arabian who sometimes is wearing a costume.

To learn more about Jackson Day, follow:

On Instagram: #imjacksonday
On Facebook: I'm Jackson Day

I'm Jackson Day and I'm Here to Stay: The True Story of a Medically Challenged Horse Who Found Fun, Friends and Fame

The photo of Jackson bowing to the flag on page 30 is by Wolfspirit Photographers and was taken as his tribute to 9/11.

Published by Somerspoint Press
978-0-692-18941-2

CPSIA information can be obtained at www.ICGtesting.com
Printed in the USA
BVIW120029021218
534166BV00001B/3